LAND USE

CLASSIFICATION MANUAL

DEVELOPED BY THE LAND CLASSIFICATION
ADVISORY COMMITTEE OF THE
DETROIT METROPOLITAN AREA

PUBLIC ADMINISTRATION SERVICE

1313 East Sixtieth Street, Chicago 37, Illinois

Printed in the United States of America

FOREWORD

In the early years of any art the practitioners must struggle to perfect their techniques—but without proper tools. Planning practitioners are just now beginning to see their art move out of the primitive stage into a more sophisticated era. For planning as we know it in the United States is still young, slightly over a half century old if we date its birth with the Burnham Plan for San Francisco.

As part of planning's maturing, we are now able to fashion tools that sharpen our eyes, that make our hands more skillful. But we still do not produce these tools at a rapid rate. Perhaps once each four or five years do we come up with something, some idea, some bit of insight, some book, or manual, or standard, that we can say truly adds to the effectiveness of the planner's activities.

I believe that this *Land Use Classification Manual* is one of these rare birds—the solid step forward, the really useful tool.

And I think what appeals to me most about the manual is that I know it is practical, usable, the distilled results of a lot of work by a lot of dirt planners, men who have slogged their way through long, detailed, and often tedious land use studies. This is the kind of tool they needed but did not have. So they invented it!

It will not be the last word in guides to land use classification. Man will devise new land uses that have not been dreamed of in heaven or on earth, or by the authors of this manual. Still in all, the system is arranged so that even an undreamt of land use can be slipped into place.

So I am pleased to have the opportunity to recommend this manual to all planners struggling with that most basic of problems, the land use plan. I know that it will avoid for them many hours of worrisome labor.

DENNIS O'HARROW, *Executive Director*
American Society of Planning Officials

July 30, 1962

PREFACE

This manual offers a classification system and code of identifying numbers for use in the collection and presentation of land use data. It is designed to make possible a coherent description of the land use structure of a township, a village, a city, or a metropolitan region. The code may be used at the level of detail needed to serve the purposes of each survey.

The classification and code were originally developed by a group of planners in the Detroit metropolitan area who were dissatisfied with existing methods, in the hope that a scheme could be devised that could be universally applied. The first draft was the work of the following unofficial group: Clyde E. Cook, Oakland County Planning Commission; Bernard A. Schroll and James F. Miller, Detroit Metropolitan Area Regional Planning Commission; Howard A. Null, formerly with the Macomb County Planning Commission and now with the firm of Parkins, Rogers and Associates, Detroit; Robert S. McCargar, formerly with the Detroit City Plan Commission and now with the Center for Community Studies, Harvard Medical School, Boston; Robert M. Sparks, formerly with the Oakland County Planning Commission and now with the City of Baltimore; and Robert Warrilow, formerly with the Detroit Area Traffic Study and now with the Contra Costa County (California) Planning Commission.

The draft manual developed by this group was distributed to some 200 planning agencies and consultants throughout the United States. With each copy went a request that the manual be reviewed and that comments be directed to the committee. The many favorable responses indicated that classifying and coding land uses as suggested in the manual would permit convenient interchange of statistical data among regions, metropolitan areas, and large and small cities.

On the basis of the comments received from those who reviewed the original draft, Charles Blessing, Chairman of the Detroit Metropolitan Area Regional Planning Commission, appointed a Land Classification Advisory Committee to develop a revised manual that would incorporate the changes and additions that had been suggested. The revision permits a better description of residential uses in large cities and provides a method of categorizing vacant or unused land. The Committee has also worked out suggested color guides and screen patterns for mapping land uses.

The Committee realizes that the development of a classification system and coding scheme does not provide a panacea for all land classification problems; it seems, however, to be an initial step in the right direction.

The description of the procedures for doing a land use survey is very general. If any person or agency desires further explanations or information regarding the experience of agencies using the manual, the Committee will be pleased to be of service. The Committee also invites the comments and criticisms of those who use the manual in their land use surveys and analyses. They may be directed to the Land Classification Advisory Committee, in care of the Detroit Metropolitan Area Regional Planning Commission, 800 Cadillac Square Building, Detroit 26, Michigan. Comments also may be sent to any member of the Committee after checking for the latest address in a current AIP directory.

LAND CLASSIFICATION ADVISORY COMMITTEE

James L. Bates
City of Pontiac Planning Commission

HAROLD BLACK
Detroit City Plan Commission

Howard A. Null
Parkins, Rogers and Associates,
    Detroit

BILL G. ROWDEN
Macomb County Planning Commission

Bernard A. Schroll
Detroit Metropolitan Area Regional
    Planning Commission

Robert Smock
Detroit Area Traffic Study

James W. Thomson
Wayne State University

George F. Tomlinson
Vilican-Leman & Associates, Inc.
Southfield, Michigan

Robert Treichel
Michigan State Highway Department
Lansing

Clyde E. Cook, *Chairman*
Oakland County Planning Commission

James F. Miller, *Secretary*
Detroit Metropolitan Area Regional
    Planning Commission

July, 1962

CONTENTS

I. DEVELOPING A STANDARD LAND USE CODE

Those seeking information on land uses in a city, in a metropolitan area, or in any of the small communities that make up a metropolitan area are frequently confronted with a crazy quilt of data—or no data at all. In the cities for which information is available, some land uses have been classified by one system, some by another; some data are years old and out of date, some are new; some land uses have been inaccurately classified, and some of the data are inaccurately reported. Often, the frequently used land use categories are too general to permit detailed studies of a small area.

A land use study is difficult to make and interpret under the most satisfactory circumstances. It is likely to be a nightmare under such trying ones. With the kinds of shortcomings that often prevail, it is difficult, if not impossible, to relate information on population densities, location of employment centers, and traffic generation, for instance, to land use data. And at best only superficial comparisons can be made among land use data for different areas and cities.

Accurate, up-to-date land use information is a necessity in making wise decisions on any matters relating to the physical development of a community—decisions relating to such matters as housing needs and urban renewal; location of schools, parks, playgrounds, and cultural facilities; transportation and parking needs; opportunities for industrial expansion; and zoning. The obvious starting point in securing this information is the adoption and application of an adequate land use classification system—a set of categories and a coding system that may be used at the level of detail that will provide the information that is needed. Also, if a classification is developed that is agreeable to and used by many planning agencies, reliable data that can easily be compared will be accumulated for the cities and regions using the classification.

A land use survey produces a picture of the present to be used as a basis for planning the future. The data from the survey contribute to the development of a master plan. They are used by planning and other officials in making day-to-day decisions. They also provide needed factual information for businessmen, residents, school officials, and others in reaching decisions in their own affairs and in relation to the community.

The Detroit Committee Objectives

The prime objective of the Land Classification Advisory Committee was to work out a land use classification system that can be used easily both to indicate all of the land uses in an entire region and to analyze in detail the land uses in a small area. The Committee also wanted a code that would make it possible to compare one part of the metropolitan area with another part, or an entire metropolitan area or parts thereof with other metropolitan areas or parts thereof.

The Committee's secondary, albeit important, objectives were (1) to suggest the usefulness of committees as a means of securing cooperation in land use studies in a region; (2) to encourage planning agencies to do "trial run" land use studies, using the suggested classification system; and (3) to help prepare the basic materials that facilitate use of the code, such as the detailed index.

What a Code Should Include

The Committee, in developing the classification system, adhered to generally accepted principles for a good land use code: (1) it must be broad enough to permit classification of every land use; (2) the categories must be clearly defined and mutually exclusive; (3) the categories must be susceptible to analysis or breakdown; and (4) the code must be easy to use and it must be easy to process the information resulting from its use.

Obviously, it was necessary to develop a code that would include a category for every land use in the Detroit area. It was not necessary, however, to provide a pigeonhole for every land use. Closely related uses could be grouped, and less important uses could be lumped in a miscellaneous category under a general category: for instance, "Residential not elsewhere classified" under "Residential." On the other hand, the code should not be so closely tailored to Detroit area needs that it would be self-defeating. Land uses in other areas had to be included if it was going to be possible to make comparisons among cities and regions.

The code also had to be flexible so that it could show the degree of detail needed to reflect the importance of any given land use in the planning scheme. That is, it should be possible to show through use of the code the amount of space devoted to the use; the place of that use in the economy of the city or the region; the importance of the use as a community function; and to some degree its planning potential or "future"—as, for example, vacant land.

It was also thought necessary to provide for the classification of land on which there is no use (vacant), of land on which there is no predominant use, and of areas that have surfaces with special characteristics—lagoons, lakes, and other water areas, for example.

The classification system also should lend itself to relatively simple field and mapping procedures and to machine processing and convenient updating of data.

On the other hand, the Committee thought it was not possible to have the code reflect all of the characteristics of each land use—the amount of smoke, noise, and odor generated by an industry, or the amount and kinds of traffic generated by recreation areas, shopping centers, or schools, or the differences between a "neighborhood shopping" area and a "general commercial" area, for instance. Many of the characteristics of land uses should be studies in themselves, the Committee believed, rather than integral parts of the land use study. Even had it been possible to include such characteristics, the Committee felt it was not desirable. Inclusion of all characteristics of a piece of land would complicate the picture so much that the primary purposes of a land use study—to help determine, in the light of such factors as population and industrial changes, how much land should be allocated in the future to each land use and where each use should be located—would be lost.

The Standard Industrial Classification Code

None of the land use codes that the Committee examined met all requirements for a "standard" system of classification. The Standard Industrial Classification[1] (SIC) code, which is used to classify "establishments"[2] by type of economic activity came closest to meeting the criteria. There are reasons, however, why the Committee thought the SIC code could not be converted to a land use code.

In the first place, the SIC system uses a combination of letters and numbers for the code (A, B, C, and so on for the ten "divisions" or top categories; 20, 201, 2011, for instance, for the subcategories). But a code in which only numbers are used (2 for a major category and 20, 201, and 2011 for the subcategories, for instance) is easier to use with mechanical data processing devices, which are extremely helpful in processing the data in land use studies.

Changing the SIC letters to numbers and conforming parts of the numerical code to land use classifications were not practicable for several reasons. The SIC code is not adaptable as a land use code in that its ten divisions are not the same as the ten "major categories" that the Committee considered most useful for land use classification purposes. For instance, "Division C, Contract construction," or "Division G, Finance, insurance, and real estate," do not of themselves constitute useful major categories for land use classification, even though they are of sufficient importance in economic activities to be major categories.

The SIC code may be "collapsed" from four to two digits by dropping the digits at the right, but it is not possible to go farther because the SIC does not provide distinctive categories at the one-digit level. For instance, 1 includes mining (10-14), contract construction (15-17), and ordnance manufacturing (19).

Another shortcoming of the SIC code as far as land use classification is concerned is that it makes no provision for mixed uses, simply because economic activities are not "mixed" in the same sense that land uses are. Frequently there is more than one use made of a parcel of land or more than one use housed in a single building. Nor is unused space (unused water area, derelict land, and vacant land and structures) classified in the SIC code, since it is not the basis for an economic activity. Both mixed uses and vacant land are important land use classifications, however, and should be accounted for in land use studies and maps.

Thus it is difficult, and in some categories, impossible, to convert the SIC code to a land use code because it is geared to economic activities—not to land uses. Lack of comparability may be pointed up, for example, in the consideration of a junkyard as an economic activity and as a land use. As an economic activity a junkyard is only a detail of another economic activity and, consequently, in the SIC code it is given a four-digit classification (5093). As a land use, it is of sufficient importance to be given a two-digit code designation (18).

There would have been a number of advantages in converting the SIC code had it been feasible. Since it

[1]U. S. Bureau of the Budget, *Standard Industrial Classification Manual* (Washington, D. C.: U. S. Government Printing Office, 1957), 433 pp. Prepared by the Technical Committee on Industrial Classification, Office of Statistical Standards. For sale by the Superintendent of Documents, U. S. Government Printing Office, Washington 25, D. C., $2.50.

[2]"Establishment" is defined in the *SIC Manual* as "an economic unit which produces goods or services—for example, a farm, a mine, a factory, a store."

was not, the Committee borrowed ideas from it liberally in devising its own code. In particular, the Committee has used as fully as possible the SIC subcategory *titles* at all levels for the land use code and also has followed generally the SIC *order of listing* subcategories. And because it is useful for planners to know what economic activity or "establishment" category a land use is in, SIC code numbers are indicated in the classification for comparable uses.

The Land Use Code

The land use coding scheme devised by the Committee starts with one-digit categories, each of which can be broken down to two-, three-, and four-digit categories —or even further if desired. At the one-digit level there are ten categories[3] (0 through 9); at the two-digit level there are potentially 100 subcategories (00 through 99); at the three-digit level, 1,000 subcategories (000 through 999); and at the four-digit level, 10,000 subcategories (0000 through 9999). In the coding scheme the number used for a basic category is also used as the first number of each of its subcategories. That is, all subcategories of category 1 at whatever level have code numbers starting with 1; all subcategories of category 2 have code numbers starting with 2; and so on.

The basic categories and their code numbers are:

0—Residential
1—Extractive and Industrial Nonmanufacturing
2—Manufacturing
3—Manufacturing
4—Transportation, Communications, and Utilities
5—Commercial
6—Personal, Business, and Professional Services
7—Public and Quasi-Public Services
8—Recreation
9—Unused Space

Each of these categories is divided into two-digit categories. For instance, for the Residential category, the subcategories and numbers are:

0-RESIDENTIAL

01—Single-family dwellings
02—Two-family dwellings
03—Three- and four-family dwellings
04—Five- to eight-family dwellings
05—Nine- or more family dwellings
06—Boarding, rooming, and fraternity houses
07—Hotels, motels, and tourist homes

---

[3]There are actually only nine categories. Manufacturing has been assigned two numbers because it has so many subcategories at the two-digit level that it is not possible to include them all under one category.

08—Mobile home parks
09—Residential not elsewhere classified

It is possible to classify one land use at one level and other land uses at different levels. In fact, in the suggested code all basic categories except Residential are broken down generally to the three-digit level and most three-digit categories are further subdivided to the four-digit level. For instance:

2-MANUFACTURING

20—Food and kindred products
201—Meat products
2011—Meat packing plants
2013—Sausages and other prepared meat products
2015—Poultry and small game dressing and packing, wholesale
202—Dairy products
2021—Creamery butter
Etc.

If there is a land use within a Manufacturing category that should be shown in even greater detail, it can be broken down to a five-digit level. How detailed the breakdown is depends to some extent on how important the land use is locally. In the Detroit area, for example, the automotive industry probably needs to be classified in considerable detail—at the three- and four-digit levels. In another area the automotive industry might be so small a factor in the local economy that it would require little breakdown.

The code, then, can be used to classify land uses at whatever degree of detail is desired. For most purposes the one-digit level is too general; the two-digit level provides considerable detail; and the three- and four-digit levels provide detailed product and service classifications.

A code that permits reporting data in detail or in general makes it possible to collect detailed information and then analyze it at the level that best suits each particular need. One agency may need a great deal of detail on certain land uses; another may need only an overall picture of that same land use. A code that can logically be expanded serves the needs of both.

The Problem of Mixed Uses

In any land use survey there will be a problem of mixed uses, and a decision must be reached on how to record them. Mixtures are found even at the parcel level, which is a relatively small unit of analysis—e.g., in an office building.

Mixed uses may be handled in several different ways:

1. Code mixtures at a higher level of generality. The shortcoming of this method is that mixtures of two or

more basically different functions cannot be so coded. And where this method can be used, information that may be needed later is lost in the process.

2. Provide categories for mixtures. The difficulty here is that so many different mixtures must be provided for.

3. Code the area according to its predominant use. This method is easier to apply than either of the first two; it is particularly good when all the activities contribute to or form parts of the major activity on the land. Where it is difficult to determine which is the predominant use, the land should be classified in the most extensive or otherwise descriptive category of land use. The shortcoming of this method is that it loses the specific character of the mix, though in doing the survey it is possible to note the fact that a mixed use exists.

4. Use multiple codes for mixtures.

5. Use multiple cards for mixtures.

The fourth and fifth possibilities are similar. In one case the multiple entries are made on the same punched card; in the other, they are made on two or more cards. These methods can be combined with the third by making the predominant use the first entry.

The Committee does not make a recommendation on the method to be adopted, although the code it has developed does not provide categories for mixtures and it recognizes that not all mixtures can be coded at a higher level of generality.

II. USING THE CODE

The agency about to undertake a land use survey needs to canvass its resources and make decisions on a number of interrelated questions. It should consider the level of detail at which various kinds of information are needed and ascertain how much of this information is already available in usable form in the files and reports of its own and other offices. It must develop a schedule of work, taking into account the funds, personnel, and time that may be devoted to the survey. It should outline, so far as possible, the field and office procedures to be followed and should try to foresee the various uses to which the land use information will be put and the ways this information should be processed and presented to serve these uses.

Preliminary Actions and Decisions

Although most professional staffs will work out their own procedures for using the code, some pointers may be useful:

1. Find out what information is already available. Large users of establishments data, using the SIC code, may have collected and organized much basic information that can be converted to the land use code.[4] For instance, decks of establishments cards are available for most, if not all, of the Detroit metropolitan area.[5] Local agencies may find that much of the information they need has already been collected by planning or other agencies at higher levels. Much useful information may also have been collected by agencies responsible for utility billing, assessment and tax billing, school census, and title and deed registration.[6] It will also be helpful if those planning a survey consult with others who have used the code; therefore, determine whether any other agency in the area—planning or otherwise—has used the code to make a land use study and, if so, what the experience with it has been.

2. Select the unit (or units) for which data are to be collected and summarized. It is not necessary to use the same unit for the entire area surveyed, either in collecting or in summarizing information. Usually the smallest unit for which data are collected is the ownership parcel or some combination of parcels, although the ownership parcel may be broken down in unusual cases (e.g., large industrial sites). Once the basic data are collected, they may be summarized for larger areas—block frontages, blocks, census tracts, and sections. Where the uses are heterogeneous, as in areas where land use patterns are changing, it may be desirable to summarize data at the parcel level; where uses are alike over a large area, as in open farmland, it may be better for summarizing purposes to use units even larger than the basic area selected.

3. Devise a system for identifying numerically the data collection and summarization units. Census tract and block numbers have already been assigned in many areas.

---

[4]Eventually, the major consumers of land use data will collect and record such data for an entire metropolitan or regional area. They will identify on cards all establishments by address, block and tract, SIC code, and land use code. A local agency can then reproduce the cards that refer to its area.

[5]All of the cards containing information of one kind are a deck.

---

[6]Such agencies might also be willing to cooperate with the planning agency by incorporating its land use classification code into their procedures in a way to contribute to keeping land use records current.

4. Decide at what level land uses are to be studied, keeping in mind that if the code is used at too general a level it overemphasizes homogeneity of land use and is misleading. It is not necessary to study each of the ten major use categories or all major subcategories or all land areas in the same degree of detail. It may be desirable, for example, to study manufacturing areas or the central business district or a redevelopment area in more detail than outdoor recreation areas. Also, more detailed levels than four digits may be required to reveal needed information for some uses.

5. Decide how and the extent to which mixed uses are to be recorded. It will probably be possible to record such uses only on large-scale maps.

The following suggestions are offered for consideration:

a. Where a lot or other basic area is divided between two or more uses at the ground level, show the actual area devoted to each use.

b. Where different uses exist on the first and upper floors, divide the lot by a diagonal line and record the first-floor use in the triangle that has the street frontage and the second-floor use in the other triangle. If it is desired to indicate other uses existing on higher floors, further divide the triangle reserved for the second-floor use and decide which part of the area is to be used for each floor. (The scale of the map will determine, of course, the extent to which this subdivision may be carried.)[7]

6. Decide generally how the information gathered in the field survey is to be tabulated. Data can be tabulated by hand or punched on cards for mechanical or electronic data processing. Hand tabulation is slow and should be contemplated only in smaller surveys. Punched cards normally should be used in surveys where the volume of like transactions is high, where they are so essentially alike that their treatment can be standardized, and where each transaction will normally be posted or analyzed in several records or reports. Data punched on cards are flexible, and if wise decisions have been made on what is gathered and recorded on the cards, the summary information that is desired can be produced easily and quickly.

Each prospective user must make his own decision on whether to use punched card methods and, if he decides to use them and does not have the needed equipment, on whether to purchase, borrow, or rent it. He will need to do some hard work before making a decision—design procedures; estimate the volume of work; estimate machine, personnel, equipment, space, and other requirements; and estimate costs. In reaching his decision, he should seek the advice of a competent technician. Manufacturers' sales representatives usually are competent technicians with wide experience who can analyze a prospective installation and help determine its cost. A present user of equipment, particularly in the same kind of work, is another good source. Management consultants or public accountants, too, are often versed in the uses of punched card equipment.[8] Data processing procedures are discussed in a later section of this manual.

For maximum efficiency if tabulating machines are used, a tentative punched card layout should be devised with the help of someone versed in machine work at the time the planning for data collection is done. The wrong approach to machine processing is to collect data and then ask how machines can be used to process them.

7. Decide generally what uses will be made of the data and how they will be presented to accomplish these uses best. Map making is discussed and some references on chart making and report writing and reproduction are listed in a later section of this manual.

It is recognized that rarely do those responsible for planning have all the information they need to make a decision free from error, or the time and funds needed to collect such information. They have to establish cutoff points—to decide that certain information is "good enough." On the other hand, if in gathering data the code is used at too general a level, information that is needed later may not be available and follow-up field work will have to be done.

In reaching a decision on the level(s) at which to use the code there is merit in thinking not of *a* land use code, *a* land use map, and *a* land use report, but of *many* codes, *many* maps, and *many* reports, each stressing the characteristics to be considered in making particular planning decisions.

Securing Maps

Secure or prepare the necessary base map or maps, making certain that the area identifications referred to in 3 above are on the maps and that maps are of a

---

[7]Further suggestions for recording mixed and special uses are given in E. B. Wilkens, *Mapping for Planning: A Procedural Guide for the Classification and Mapping of Land Uses and Related Technical Studies.* Chicago: Public Administration Service, 1948. 25 pp. mimeo. $1.50. The land use categories and mapping colors suggested in the present manual generally parallel those recommended in this earlier manual but are much more detailed.

[8]For a general introduction to the use of punched cards, see Burton Dean Friedman, *Punched Card Primer.* Chicago: Public Administration Service, 1955. 85 pp. $3.50.

scale large enough that the desired information may be recorded on them. These maps will show lot or property lines, blocks, streets, highways, railroads, rivers, streams, and sometimes buildings and major uses.

Satisfactory maps may be available from the city or county engineer's, assessor's, or clerk's offices, a local utility, a private map company, or other source. If satisfactory base maps are not available, they will have to be constructed, using such resources as records of survey plats, usually filed in the office of the registrar of deeds; county aerial photographic survey maps and the aerial maps of state highway, conservation, and other agencies; U. S. Geological Survey maps; and public or private topographic-engineering surveys.

Maps of several scales may be needed, depending on the degree of detail at which information is gathered and presented.

Field Work

The field work can be done by planning technicians, if there are enough of them. It can also be done by untrained workers if they are carefully selected, are given some advance training, and are supervised by professionals. It is important that the field staff be large enough that the survey can be carried forward steadily and completed quickly.

Before field work is begun the public should be alerted to the fact that the survey is to be made and should be told about its purposes and procedures. A notice may be inserted in the local newspapers; if the city has a radio or television program, the survey may be described on it; or notices may be included with utility bills.

In preparing for and doing field work, the following steps are suggested:

1. Divide the area to be studied into convenient sections.

2. Assign one field worker to a section if the work is to be done on foot; assign two to a section if it is to be done by car.

3. Equip field workers with an identification card, letter, or badge, a base map of the section folded on a clipboard, pencils, and a copy of the land use classification code.

4. Call a meeting of all field workers and supervisory staff at which the supervisor in charge describes the purposes and procedures of the survey—stressing such matters as the proper approach of the worker to property users, the importance of systematic and complete coverage of all areas and full and accurate recording of uses, the method of recording mixed uses and vacant land and buildings, and the desirability of raising questions when in doubt about any use or procedure. Pay special attention to the importance of discovering and noting exceptional and nonconforming uses. Also call attention to the information on uses to be secured from such sources as the number of door bells, mail boxes, and utility meters at a building, from utility company records, and from city directories.

5. Have each worker do a trial run of perhaps a half-day in his section. He should then return to the office so that he may raise questions and a check may be made on whether he is using the code correctly so that procedures may be evaluated to see if any changes are needed.

6. Determine on the basis of the trial run whether the field staff is large enough and whether it is assigned most efficiently. For example, two trained workers can cover several square miles of rural or semirural area or of area devoted entirely or largely to a single use (such as a subdivision) by car in a day, but it may take one person a day to cover a few blocks in high-density areas on foot.

7. Record information on the maps by writing in
    a. the full name of the use,
    b. an abbreviation of or an appropriate symbol for some kinds of uses, or
    c. the appropriate code number.
There is less likelihood of error if the name of the use or an abbreviated name is recorded. All workers should use the same method of recording. Also record
    d. the name of the establishment for all industrial and commercial uses.

8. As an alternative to 7, record the information directly on the data processing cards. For information on this procedure, secure the advice of the local data processing equipment representative.

Office Work

As field work on sections of the base map is completed, they should be deposited in the office. There the recorded data should be checked promptly against other sources of information so that the field worker can explain discrepancies and correct errors either from his memory of the parcel or by rechecking. Sources of information include, among others, United States Geological Survey maps, Sanborn maps, aerial photographs, highway maps, city maps and directories, assessors' tax maps, and utility records.

Office work will include the following steps:

1. Enter the standard land use classification code numbers on the base map, if they have not been entered during the survey.

2. Convert all parcel measurements to acres and

record the acreage on the base map if space permits; record it also on the card that is made to record other information for each parcel.

3. If data are to be tabulated by hand, prepare the work sheets on which they are to be summarized and make the entries.

4. If data are to be hand sorted from cards, enter the use on the card, punch along the edge of the card the space assigned to the use code number, and sort the cards either visually or with a needle to secure the desired tabulations.[9]

5. In case of machine tabulation:

a. Enter the measurements, coding, and other information for each parcel on the punched cards directly or on sheets from which they will be punched.

b. Introduce into the cards or sheets any desired ratings or additional information, such as planning area types.

c. Punch cards.

d. Verify accuracy in entering data on cards.

e. Reach final decisions on the desired tabulations and run them.

6. For making tables, use duplicated sheets on which the column heads have been entered. These sheets may be typed with carbon copies, mimeographed, or reproduced by photo offset.

7. Reach final decisions on the maps that are desired and on how they are to be made and reproduced. Maps may include:

a. A large-scale color display map for office reference and for making presentations at city council meetings, public hearings, or citizen meetings. The scale will depend on the size of the community. If the base map or maps used in field work cannot be used for this purpose, a blueprint office can make a map of the size desired.

b. A sectional atlas for office reference.

c. A land use map of smaller size that shows less detail than a.

d. Analytical maps of less detail to be used for special areas and purposes.

8. Reach decisions on the data that are to be charted and make the charts.

9. Write, reproduce, and distribute the report or reports.

10. Reach tentative decisions on the frequency and methods of updating land use information.

---

[9]This keysort method is described, with illustrations, in Warren (Michigan) Planning Commission. *Existing Land Use.* 1961. 42 pp. Appendix. (Master Plan Series, vol. II.) This is the first completed study using the code of the Detroit area Land Classification Advisory Committee. It contains valuable information on the gathering and processing of data and examples of their uses. It is also an example of an attractive report entirely reproduced, by multilith, by the planning staff.

III. REPORTING RESULTS

When field and office work of the land use classification survey have been completed, attention is turned to reporting the results. Questions relating to reporting have arisen, of course, at various stages of the survey, and some decisions or tentative decisions have doubtless been reached. Others are still to be made.

Reporting involves writing both descriptive and analytical text; making maps, charts, and tables; and reproducing and distributing reports. Some of this reporting is for use only within the planning or other governmental offices; some of it is for distribution to offices, agencies, and individuals outside the government. In preparing reports the audience(s) to which they are directed affect style of writing, amounts and kinds of illustrations, format, and method of reproduction. The method of reproducing maps and reports needs to be decided before any graphic materials, or even final text, have been prepared. The number of copies required, the quality of product desired, costs, staff time required, and the machines readily available all affect the decision.

It is not within the scope of this manual to make suggestions on text writing, chart making, construction of tables, and report reproduction. Each is a subject for a manual in itself. A few of the many helpful books and pamphlets to which authors and others responsible for reporting may turn if they wish to supplement their own experience are listed below. Following this listing is a brief discussion of the principles and procedures of map making. Well constructed maps are perhaps the best way to show patterns and relationships of land uses. Wide adoption of the colors or screen patterns suggested for the several land uses will further one of the Committee's objectives—the comparison not only of the parts of one metropolitan area but of an entire metropolitan area or parts thereof with other metropolitan areas or parts thereof.

Some Reporting Tools

Of the many books and pamphlets on report writing and reproduction, five are here suggested. Each will be useful for the purposes indicated in the title and annotation.

The Royal Bank of Canada. *The Communication of Ideas*. Montreal: The Bank, February, 1959.

This publication is a compilation of 12 *Monthly Letters*—lively, short essays "dealing with the problem of making ourselves understood one to another." Some of the titles are: "On Saying What You Mean," "Writing a Report," "On Writing Briefly," "On Writing Clearly," "About Style in Writing," and "The Right Word."

Crosby, Alexander L. *Pamphlets: How to Write & Print Them*. National Publicity Council for Health and Welfare Services, Inc., 257 Fourth Avenue, New York 10, New York, 1959. 32 pp., illus. $1.25.

Covers such matters as framework and facts, putting life into print, estimating space, choosing text type, layout and art, printing services, a table of relative printing costs, and economizing.

Melcher, Daniel and Nancy Larrick. *Printing and Promotion Handbook; How to Plan, Produce, and Use Printing, Advertising, and Direct Mail*. 2d ed. New York: McGraw-Hill Book Co., 1956. 438 pp., illus. $7.00.

Arranged in the form of an encyclopedia, this is a practical reference book on how to plan and produce various kinds of printed materials, how to choose the right process and printer, the major printing and office duplicating processes, the use of cuts and plates, designing and illustrating, editing and proofreading, selecting paper, and other problems. Contains samples of type faces.

Douglass, Paul. *Communication through Reports*. Englewood Cliffs, N. J.: Prentice-Hall, Inc., 1957. 410 pp., illus. $6.00.

This reference book describes the many kinds of reports; the building of clear, readable reports through words, sentences, paragraphs, and punctuation; and the use of tables and charts.

Flesch, Rudolf. *How to Write, Speak, and Think More Effectively*. New York: Harper & Bros., 1960. 362 pp., $4.95.

Gives a scientifically tested system designed to improve three main mental activities—writing, speaking, and thinking.

The following books, all amply illustrated, contain much practical information on the use, making, and reproduction of charts, graphs, and other pictorial material.

Rogers, Anna C. *Graphic Charts Handbook*. Washington, D. C.: Public Affairs Press 1961. 190 pp. $6.00.

Describes chart planning and the making of the many kinds of charts, as well as statistical maps and pictographs. Contains a section on methods of reproducing graphic materials.

Spear, Mary Eleanor. *Charting Statistics*. New York: McGraw-Hill Book Co., Inc., 1952. 253 pp. $4.50.

An introduction to graphic presentation and the many kinds of charts. Contains a chapter on duplicating.

Modley, Rudolf and Dyno Lowenstein. *Pictographs and Graphs; How to Make and Use Them*. New York: Harper and Bros., 1952. 186 pp. $4.00.

Covers charting, with emphasis on the pictograph. Has a chapter on tools and one on preparing artwork for reproduction.

Many paper companies and printing establishments issue reference guides that are helpful to the producer and publisher of reports. Two are here cited.

The Pocket Pal. 4th ed. International Paper Co., 220 East 42d Street, New York, New York, 1963. $0.50.

Describes printing processes, composition, and printers' measurements. Contains sections on proofreaders' marks, word division, copy fitting, marking up copy, photoengraving, printing inks, and graphic arts terms. Also contains practical information on paper quality and selection.

Book Publishers' Guide; A Manual on the Selection of Paper and the Design and Production of Bound Books. 2d ed. Oxford Paper Company, 230 Park Avenue, New York 17, New York, 1960. 65 pp., appendixes. $5.00.

Contains short essays on book production and letterpress and offset printing. Describes the manufacture and selection of book papers and has sample pages of many kinds and weights of papers. Has a book making flow chart, a book paper selector chart, and a list of proofreaders' and editorial marks.

Printers are glad to help with problems of book design, the selection of type faces and sizes, paper, inks, and other publishing questions. They will furnish books that illustrate the type faces they stock and will set sample pages ahead of printing.

The writer of reports will need a standard dictionary on his desk for ready reference. If his organization issues a style manual, he will also have a copy at hand. If it does not, he will find one of the style manuals issued by university or other presses a useful reference tool.

Making Maps

In making maps initial decisions must be reached on base materials, drafting tools or media, and methods of reproduction. The uses to which the maps will be put, the emphasis desired, the staff available, costs, number of copies, and available reproduction methods will affect these decisions. The application of general principles of good mapping will contribute to the effectiveness of the finished product.

Mapping Principles. Maps should be accurate, clear, legible, and well arranged.

The base maps and the information added to them must be accurate. The amount of detail they show will depend on the scale of the maps and the method of presentation. The dimensions of the maps must be correct and they must show water bodies, streets, and other map elements accurately. The information that is added with lines and other means also must be accurate. Any generalized areas not precisely located should be of a shape or outline that will not be associated with a precise location.

The data or the proposals that are mapped must be clearly presented in order to be understood and correctly interpreted. The uses that are presented on any one map should be limited to the number that can be depicted clearly, and irrelevant detail that does not add to the presentation should not be included. Each completed map, although it may be part of a series of maps or of a text presentation, should be fully explanatory in itself. It should carry a legend that identifies each color, pattern, or symbol. The map should be clearly titled and should show scale, northpoint, the date when the information was collected, and the name of the agency preparing the map.

A map should be readable. The information on it must be shown large enough to be readily seen. Size, of course, is tied directly to the scale of the map. The use of familiar symbols also contributes to readability. An example is the common line symbol used to indicate railroads. Contrast also contributes to readability—contrast in lines, colors, or screen patterns used to depict the elements shown on the map.

Lines are differentiated by weight and design. Lines must compete for attention with colors or patterns, and the selection of line weights and designs must be related to these factors and to the principal uses intended for the map. Lines may be solid or they may consist of dashes of various lengths, dots of various sizes, or some combination of these or other elements. In determining widths of lines, assign the finest to the least important elements and grade up to the most important.

Major contrasts may be obtained through the use of color. The distance at which a map will be viewed affects the degree to which colors and hues of colors will stand out. Generally, and to the degree possible in land use mapping, large areas in a single use should be shown in a subdued color or hue; land uses that are to be emphasized should be in more intense or brilliant colors or hues. Each major land use classification should be assigned a basic color, and if sub-classifications are to be shown they should be assigned hues of this same color. If the more detailed use groups within a category range in intensity, hues that are darker or more vivid should be used to show the more intense uses.

Contrast among areas can also be obtained through the use of screen patterns. Screens should be chosen that stand out from each other at the distance from which the map will be read. In using screens the following principles should be followed so far as is possible. Large areas in one use should be shown with a less conspicuous screen. Land uses of small area should be depicted in a distinctive pattern that stands out. When the size of a use area is too small to be represented clearly by a screen it may be shown with a symbol. Land uses that are separated into component parts, e.g., densities of residential land, should have the same general screen pattern, with the more intense uses having the denser or darker screens. Screens may suggest the classification they represent, as a woods screen for recreation areas.

The size and shape of the map sheet are determined by the area to be mapped, the scale, and possible future reproduction in reduced size. Generally, rectangular maps whose sides are in the ratio 3:5 are most stable and visually pleasing.

Composition, or the arrangement of the map elements, is a key factor in effective presentation. The features of the map on which attention is to be centered should appear as near the visual center of the sheet as possible. The visual center of a rectangular sheet is located at about 5 per cent of the height of the sheet above the actual center. To the degree possible, other elements depicted by the map should be balanced around the visual center according to their area and visual weight.

The placing of the identifying information—title, scale, legend, northpoint symbol, and notes—also affect the appearance and readability of the map. These items should be blocked out on paper and tried in various locations to determine where they fit best.

Base Materials. The type and weight of the base material selected for a given job will depend on the durability needed, the drafting tools or media to be used, the dimensional stability (resistance to stretch, shrink, and curl) required, and the reproduction method to be employed. Base materials for mapping include paper, board, cloth, acetate, and stabilene film.

Papers are available in a wide range of sizes, weights, strengths, textures, and surface qualities. They fall into the general categories of opaque and transparent. Primary considerations in selecting paper are the uses contemplated for the finished drawing and the methods of making and reproducing it. If photographic reproduction is contemplated, the whiter the paper the better the negative.

A variety of tracing papers are available in several weights and degrees of transparency. Generally, tracing papers that have been chemically treated are stronger and more durable than natural tracing papers, but they are more expensive. Vellum is a superior quality tracing paper that takes ink readily and is very strong. It has high rag content and is chemically treated to give it a high degree of transparency.

Before selecting papers, samples should be tested to see how various media work on them. Some papers do not take ink; others do not take colored pencil; others do not respond well to other media.

Illustration board is used for finished presentations when a more durable base material than paper is needed. Many papers do not take erasures well and if scratched lose their surface quality so that work cannot be done on them again. Boards, being multiple-ply materials of uniform quality throughout, usually take erasures successfully.

Tracing cloth is a fine linen or cotton cloth, sized to accept pencil or ink work. Blue cloth is usually used for ink drawing; white cloth may be used for either pencil or ink work. Tracing cloth is highly transparent and scale distortion is held to a minimum. It is commonly used for precision drafting from which many reproductions are to be made or for maps that are to be retained for a long time.

Acetate is a cellulose material available with either a smooth or a matte (dull) surface and in a wide range of thicknesses. The most effective use of acetate is in overlay work. Smooth surface acetates require special acetate inks, whereas pencil or India ink can be used on the matte surface. Transparent screens such as Zip-a-Tone can also be applied to acetate.

Stabilene film consists of a transparent synthetic base to which is added either a pencil-and-ink or a scribe-coat surface. Stabilene film is an outstanding base material for accurate mapping; it is high in dimensional stability, transparency, flexibility, and resistance to tearing.

Stabilene film with scribe-coat surface is especially good for use in producing multicolor maps, as the dimensional stability of the film permits perfect registration of the plates containing the various colors. A scribing instrument is used to remove the scribe coat from the film where lines or other images are to appear. The finished drawing then becomes a negative.

Drafting on stabilene film is done with scribing instruments and can be completed considerably faster than pen and ink work. Corrections or revisions involve the use of a correction fluid rather than scraping or erasing. Commercial scribers are available, but they are expensive. Improvised scribing instruments such as a compass and divider points or phonograph needles can be used successfully to produce the sharp, clean lines necessary for good reproduction.

Drafting Media. Land use mapping involves differentiation among the various use types, and the most readable way to show this differentiation is by color. It may also be shown by screen pattern, and maps done in screen pattern are less costly to reproduce. Symbols may be used along with colors to show special uses, such as locations of governmental offices, churches, parks, and so on. Symbols, letters, names, or cross-hatching may be imposed on color to achieve greater detail.

Either a basic color or a basic screen pattern may be expanded when it is desired to show more detailed differentiations or gradations in use—for example, in mapping fairly small areas in order to consider requests for zoning changes.

Need for expansion of a basic color or pattern is more apt to occur for some uses than for others—housing, for example. Also, in areas in which there are high concentrations of a basic use, it may be desired to expand the color or pattern to show gradations of it for special purposes. Examples might be the kinds of government offices in the District of Columbia, specific uses in aircraft manufacturing in the Los Angeles area, or uses relating to automobile manufacturing in Detroit.

The use of maps differs from that of tables and other numerical presentations for land use analysis. Generally, there will be less breakdown of the code when using colors or screens for visual presentation than when analysis is being done with machine tabulations. From the visual point of view, the interest is apt to be in sizable blocks of use, as in industrial areas when studying the journey to work. Probably only part of the uses (colors or screens) will be shown on any one map, though many planning offices do prepare one large map showing all the basic uses for office display. For large areas in many uses, however, it is not possible to show all uses distinctly no matter what the size of the map. Sometimes for maps in color, related land uses are combined into one category in order to reduce the number of colors. In such cases the distinction between original categories can be maintained by the use of cross-hatching.

The accompanying chart suggests colors and screen patterns. The pencil colors and numbers are for Eagle Pencil Company Prismacolor pencils. They are colors widely used by planning agencies to show the land uses indicated. An agency may need to add to these colors for its specific needs. This brand, the Dixon Pencil Company Thinex, and some others provide a wide range of colors for mapping work. Before adoption, each color should be tested on a piece of the base material, since it is difficult to apply some colors evenly and some base materials will not take all colors in the same degree of evenness. In presenting data, colored pencils are used at full weight or value to insure uniformity and thus avoid confusion in interpretation.

Prepared screens consist of patterns, symbols, and solid colors printed on transparent film with an adhesive backing. Screens make possible sharp, clear, precise, and inexpensive reproductions and their use involves a minimum of skill. Pieces are cut to size with a needle, small knife, or other sharp instrument and rubbed into position on the map.

Before selecting a screen product the method of reproducing maps must be known, since the backing of some screens is affected by heat and some reproduction processes involve the use of heat. Also, some backings are pressure sensitive and once these screens are placed on a map it is difficult, and sometimes impossible, to remove them. It is therefore a good idea to try out samples before adoption.

A major difficulty in using prepared screens lies in securing a series of patterns that show varying degrees of intensity, density, value, or other characteristics, particularly when reduced. The chart will serve as a guide in the selection of screen patterns that show differences effectively even when considerably reduced. The patterns and numbers are for Zip-a-Tone, one of the screen products most commonly used for mapping. It is manufactured by Para-Tone, Inc., which also produces Blu-Zip, another screen often used in mapping. Still another is Contak film, which also offers a good range of patterns.

LAND USE CLASSIFICATION COLOR AND SCREEN GUIDE

PENCIL NUMBER*	COLOR	CODE CATEGORY	LAND USE	CODE CATEGORY	SCREEN	PATTERN NUMBER**
918		0	Residential	0		18
913		1	Agriculture	1		304
936		1	Extractive	1		364
967		1	Industrial nonmanufacturing	1		564R
935		2-3	Manufacturing	2-3		Solid Black
931		4	Transportation	4		433
924		5	Commercial	5		330
903		7	Public and quasi-public	7		320
909		8	Recreation	8		647
938		9	Unused space	9		White

Example of expansion of color and screen for Residential land use.

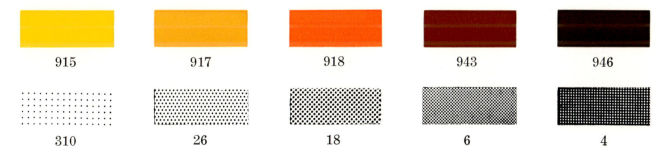

915	917	918	943	946
310	26	18	6	4

*Prismacolor pencil, Eagle Pencil Company

**Zip-a-Tone, Para-Tone, Inc.

Reprinted from *Land Use Classification Manual*, developed by the Land Classification Advisory Committee of the Detroit Metropolitan Area. (Public Administration Service, 1313 East 60th Street, Chicago 37, Illinois, 1962).

LAND USE
CLASSIFICATION AND CODE

0   RESIDENTIAL

    01   Single-family dwellings 88

    02   Two-family dwellings 88

    03   Three- and four-family dwellings 88

    04   Five- to eight-family dwellings 88

    05   Nine- or more family dwellings 88

    06   Boarding, rooming, and fraternity houses 702, 704

    07   Hotels, motels, and tourist homes 7011, 7012, 7013

    08   Mobile home parks 7031

    09   Residential not elsewhere classified 88

1   EXTRACTIVE AND INDUSTRIAL NONMANUFACTURING

    10   Agriculture 01, 02

        101   Field crop farms 011
            1013   Cash grain farms 0113
            1019   Other field crop farms 0119

        102   Fruit, tree nut, and vegetable farms 012
            1022   Fruit and tree nut farms 0122
            1023   Vegetable farms 0123

        103   Livestock farms 013
            1032   Dairy farms 0132
            1033   Poultry farms 0133
            1039   Livestock farms not elsewhere classified 0139

        104   General farms 014
            1042   General farms primarily crop 0142
            1043   General farms primarily livestock 0143
            1044   General crop and livestock farms 0144

        108   Noncommercial farms 021
            1082   Part-time farms 0212
            1083   Residential farms 0213
            1084   Institutional farms 0214

    11   Agricultural services and hunting and trapping 07

NOTE: The code numbers established by the Committee are shown at the left. Corresponding SIC code numbers at the two-digit level are at the right. Also shown at the right are all SIC code numbers at the three- and four-digit levels that *differ* from Committee code numbers. - - - indicates there is no exactly corresponding SIC category. It will be noted that, for the most part, the Committee's groups 2, 3, 4, and 5 are taken directly from the SIC manual.

177   Concrete work

178   Water well drilling

179   Miscellaneous special trade contractors
    1791   Structural steel erection
    1792   Ornamental metal work
    1793   Glass and glazing work
    1794   Excavating and foundation work
    1795   Wrecking and demolition work
    1796   Installation or erection of building equipment not elsewhere classified
    1799   Special trade contractors not elsewhere classified

18   Junk yards—scrap and waste wholesaling 5093

19   Other industrial nonmanufacturing not elsewhere classified ..... - - -

2   MANUFACTURING

20   Food and kindred products 20

   201   Meat products
    2011   Meat packing plants
    2013   Sausages and other prepared meat products
    2015   Poultry and small game dressing and packing, wholesale

   202   Dairy products
    2021   Creamery butter
    2022   Natural cheese
    2023   Condensed and evaporated milk
    2024   Ice cream and frozen desserts
    2025   Special dairy products
    2026   Fluid milk processing and distributing

   203   Canning and preserving fruits, vegetables, and seafoods
    2031   Canned and cured seafoods
    2032   Canned specialties
    2033   Canned fruits, vegetables, preserves, jams, and jellies
    2034   Dried and dehydrated fruits and vegetables
    2035   Pickled fruits and vegetables, vegetable sauces and seasonings, and salad dressings
    2036   Fresh or frozen packaged fish
    2037   Frozen fruits, fruit juices, vegetables, and specialties

   204   Grain mill products
    2041   Flour and other grain mill products
    2042   Prepared feeds for animals and fowls
    2043   Cereal preparations
    2044   Rice milling
    2045   Blended and prepared flour
    2046   Wet corn milling

   205   Bakery products

2051 Bread and other bakery products, except biscuits, crackers, and pretzels

2052 Biscuits, crackers, and pretzels

206 Sugar

2061 Cane sugar, except refining

2062 Cane sugar refining

2063 Beet sugar

207 Confectionery and related products

2071 Candy and other confectionery products

2072 Chocolate and cocoa products

2073 Chewing gum

208 Beverage industries

2082 Malt liquors

2083 Malt

2084 Wines, brandy, and brandy spirits

2085 Distilled, rectified, and blended liquors

2086 Bottled and canned soft drinks and carbonated waters

2087 Flavoring extracts and flavoring syrups not elsewhere classified

209 Miscellaneous food preparations and kindred products

2091 Cottonseed oil mills

2092 Soybean oil mills

2093 Vegetable oil mills, except cottonseed and soybean

2094 Grease and tallow

2095 Animal and marine fats and oils, except grease and tallow

2096 Shortening, table oils, margarine, and other edible fats and oils not elsewhere classified

2097 Manufactured ice

2098 Macaroni, spaghetti, vermicelli, and noodles

2099 Food preparations not elsewhere classified

21 Tobacco manufactures 21

211 Cigarettes

212 Cigars

213 Tobacco (chewing and smoking) and snuff

214 Tobacco stemming and redrying

22 Textile mill products 22

221 Broad woven fabric mills, cotton

222 Broad woven fabric mills, man-made fiber and silk

223 Broad woven fabric mills, wool, including dyeing and finishing

224 Narrow fabrics and other smallwares mills, cotton, wool, silk, and man-made fibers

225 Knitting mills

    2251   Full-fashioned hosiery mills
    2252   Seamless hosiery mills
    2253   Knit outerwear mills
    2254   Knit underwear mills
    2256   Knit fabric mills
    2259   Knitting mills not elsewhere classified

226   Dyeing and finishing textiles, except wool fabrics and knit goods
    2261   Finishers of broad woven cotton fabrics
    2262   Finishers of broad woven fabrics of man-made fiber and silk
    2269   Dyeing and finishing textiles not elsewhere classified

227   Floor covering mills
    2271   Woven carpets and rugs
    2272   Tufted carpets and rugs
    2279   Carpets, rugs, and mats not elsewhere classified

228   Yarn and thread mills
    2281   Yarn spinning mills for cotton, man-made fibers, and silk
    2282   Yarn throwing, twisting, and winding mills for cotton, man-made fibers, and silk
    2283   Yarn mills for wool, including carpet and rug yarn
    2284   Thread mills

229   Miscellaneous textile goods
    2291   Felt goods, except woven felts and hats
    2292   Lace goods
    2293   Paddings and upholstery filling
    2294   Processed waste and recovered fibers and flock
    2295   Artificial leather, oilcloth, and other impregnated and coated fabrics, except rubberized
    2296   Tire cord and fabric
    2297   Wool scouring, worsted combing, and tow to top mills
    2298   Cordage and twine
    2299   Textile goods not elsewhere classified

23   Apparel and other finished products made from fabrics and similar materials   23

  231   Men's, youths', and boys' suits, coats, and overcoats

  232   Men's, youths', and boys' furnishings, work clothing, and allied garments
    2321   Shirts (except work shirts), collars, and nightwear
    2322   Underwear
    2323   Neckwear
    2327   Separate trousers
    2328   Work clothing
    2329   Men's, youths', and boys' clothing not elsewhere classified

  233   Women's, misses', and juniors' outerwear
    2331   Blouses, waists, and shirts
    2335   Dresses

2337 Suits, skirts, and coats, except fur coats and raincoats
2339 Women's, misses', and juniors' outerwear not elsewhere classified

234 Women's, misses', children's, and infants' undergarments
2341 Underwear and nightwear
2342 Corsets and allied garments

235 Hats, caps, and millinery
2351 Millinery
2352 Men's and boys' hats and caps

236 Girls', children's, and infants' outerwear
2361 Dresses, blouses, waists, and shirts
2363 Coats and suits
2369 Girls', children's, and infants' outerwear not elsewhere classified

237 Fur goods

238 Miscellaneous apparel and accessories
2381 Dress and work gloves, except knit and all leather
2384 Robes and dressing gowns
2385 Raincoats and other waterproof outer garments
2386 Leather and sheep-lined clothing
2387 Apparel belts
2389 Apparel not elsewhere classified

239 Miscellaneous fabricated textile products
2391 Curtains and draperies
2392 Housefurnishings, except curtains and draperies
2393 Textile bags
2394 Canvas products
2395 Pleating, decorative and novelty stitching, and tuck-
ing for the trade
2396 Apparel findings and related products
2397 Schiffli machine embroideries
2399 Fabricated textile products not elsewhere classified

24 Lumber and wood products, except furniture 24

241 Logging camps and logging contractors

242 Sawmills and planing mills
2421 Sawmills and planing mills, general
2426 Hardwood dimension and flooring mills
2429 Special product sawmills not elsewhere classified

243 Millwork, veneer, plywood, and prefabricated structural
wood products
2431 Millwork plants
2432 Veneer and plywood plants
2433 Prefabricated wooden buildings and structural
members

244 Wooden containers
2441 Nailed and lock-corner wooden boxes and shook

         2442   Wirebound boxes and crates
         2443   Veneer and plywood containers, except boxes and crates
         2445   Cooperage

     249   Miscellaneous wood products
         2491   Wood preserving
         2499   Wood products not elsewhere classified

25   Furniture and fixtures 25

     251   Household furniture
         2511   Wood household furniture, except upholstered
         2512   Wood household furniture, upholstered
         2514   Metal household furniture
         2515   Mattresses and bedsprings
         2519   Household furniture not elsewhere classified

     252   Office furniture
         2521   Wood office furniture
         2522   Metal office furniture

     253   Public building and related furniture

     254   Partitions, shelving, lockers, and office and store fixtures
         2541   Wood partitions, shelving, lockers, and office and store fixtures
         2542   Metal partitions, shelving, lockers, and office and store fixtures

     259   Miscellaneous furniture and fixtures
         2591   Venetian blinds and shades
         2599   Furniture and fixtures not elsewhere classified

26   Paper and allied products 26

     261   Pulp mills

     262   Paper mills, except building paper mills

     263   Paperboard mills

     264   Converted paper and paperboard products, except containers and boxes
         2641   Paper coating and glazing
         2642   Envelopes
         2643   Bags, except textile bags
         2644   Wallpaper
         2645   Die-cut paper and paperboard, cardboard
         2646   Pressed and molded pulp goods
         2649   Converted paper and paperboard products not elsewhere classified

     265   Paperboard containers and boxes
         2651   Folding paperboard boxes
         2652   Set-up paperboard boxes
         2653   Corrugated and solid fiber boxes
         2654   Sanitary food containers

2655   Fiber cans, tubes, drums, and similar products

266   Building paper and building board mills

27   Printing, publishing, and allied industries   27

271   Newspaper publishing and printing

272   Periodical publishing and printing

273   Books
2731   Book publishing and printing
2732   Book printing

274   Miscellaneous publishing

275   Commercial printing
2751   Commercial printing, except lithography
2752   Lithography
2753   Engraving and plate printing

276   Manifold business forms manufacturing

277   Greeting card manufacturing

278   Bookbinding and related industries
2782   Blankbooks, loose-leaf binders and devices
2789   Bookbinding and miscellaneous related work

279   Service industries for the printing trade
2791   Typesetting
2793   Photoengraving
2794   Electrotyping and stereotyping
2799   Service industries for the printing trades not elsewhere classified

28   Chemicals and allied products   28

281   Industrial inorganic and organic chemicals
2812   Alkalies and chlorine
2813   Industrial gases
2814   Cyclic (coal tar) crudes
2815   Dyes, dye (cyclic) intermediates, and organic pigments (lakes and toners)
2816   Inorganic pigments
2818   Industrial organic chemicals not elsewhere classified
2819   Industrial inorganic chemicals not elsewhere classified

282   Plastics materials and synthetic resins, synthetic rubber,
and synthetic and other man-made fibers, except glass
2821   Plastics materials, synthetic resins, and nonvulcan-
izable elastomers
2822   Synthetic rubber (vulcanizable elastomers)
2823   Cellulosic man-made fibers
2824   Synthetic organic fibers, except cellulosic

283   Drugs
2831   Biological products

2833   Medicinal chemicals and botanical products

2834   Pharmaceutical preparations

284   Soaps, detergents, and cleaning preparations; perfumes, cosmetics, and other toilet preparations

     2841   Soaps and other detergents, except specialty cleaners

     2842   Specialty cleaning, polishing, and sanitation preparations, except soaps and detergents

     2843   Surface-active agents, finishing agents, and sulfonated oils and assistants

     2844   Perfumes, cosmetics, and other toilet preparations

285   Paints, varnishes, lacquers, enamels, and allied products

     2851   Paints, varnishes, lacquers, and enamels

     2852   Putty, caulking compounds, and allied products

286   Gum and wood chemicals

287   Agricultural chemicals

     2871   Fertilizers

     2872   Fertilizers, mixing only

     2873   Agricultural pesticides

     2879   Agricultural chemicals not elsewhere classified

289   Miscellaneous chemical products

     2891   Glue and gelatin

     2892   Explosives

     2893   Printing ink

     2894   Fatty acids

     2895   Carbon black

     2899   Chemicals and chemical preparations not elsewhere classified

29   Petroleum refining and related industries   29

    291   Petroleum refining

    295   Paving and roofing materials

     2951   Paving mixtures and blocks

     2952   Asphalt felts and coatings

    299   Miscellaneous products of petroleum and coal

     2992   Lubricating oils and greases

     2999   Products of petroleum and coal not elsewhere classified

3   MANUFACTURING

30   Rubber and miscellaneous plastics products   30

    301   Tires and tubing

    302   Rubber footwear

    303   Reclaimed rubber

    306   Fabricated rubber products not elsewhere classified

    307   Miscellaneous plastics products

31   Leather and leather products   31

     311   Leather tanning and finishing

     312   Industrial leather belting and packing

     313   Boot and shoe cut stock and findings

     314   Footwear, except rubber
         3141   Footwear, except house slippers
         3142   House slippers

     315   Gloves and mittens
         3151   Dress, semidress, and work gloves
         3152   Mittens

     316   Luggage

     317   Handbags and other personal leather goods
         3171   Women's handbags and purses
         3172   Personal leather goods, except handbags and purses

     319   Leather goods not elsewhere classified

32   Stone, clay, and glass products   32

     321   Flat glass

     322   Glass and glassware, pressed or blown
         3221   Glass containers
         3229   Pressed and blown glass and glassware not elsewhere classified

     323   Glass products made of purchased glass

     324   Cement, hydraulic

     325   Structural clay products
         3251   Brick and structural clay tile
         3253   Ceramic wall and floor tile
         3255   Clay refractories
         3259   Structural clay products not elsewhere classified

     326   Pottery and related products
         3261   Vitreous china plumbing fixtures and china and earthenware fittings and bathroom accessories
         3262   Vitreous china table and kitchen articles
         3263   Fine earthenware (whiteware) table and kitchen articles
         3264   Porcelain electrical supplies
         3269   Pottery products not elsewhere classified

     327   Concrete, gypsum, and plaster products
         3271   Concrete brick and block
         3272   Concrete products, except brick and block
         3273   Ready-mixed concrete
         3274   Lime
         3275   Gypsum products (plaster)

     328   Cut stone and stone products

329   Abrasive, asbestos, and miscellaneous nonmetallic mineral products
- 3291   Abrasive products
- 3292   Asbestos products
- 3293   Steam and other packing and pipe and boiler covering
- 3295   Minerals and earths, ground or otherwise treated
- 3296   Mineral wool
- 3297   Nonclay refractories
- 3299   Nonmetallic mineral products not elsewhere classified

33   Primary metals industries   33

331   Blast furnaces, steelworks, and rolling and finishing mills
- 3312   Blast furnaces (including coke ovens), steelworks, and rolling mills
- 3313   Electrometallurgical products
- 3315   Steel wire drawing and steel nails and spikes
- 3316   Cold rolled sheets, strips, and bars
- 3317   Steel pipe and tubes

332   Iron and steel foundries
- 3321   Gray iron foundries
- 3322   Malleable iron foundries
- 3323   Steel foundries

333   Primary smelting and refining of nonferrous metals
- 3331   Primary smelting and refining of copper
- 3332   Primary smelting and refining of lead
- 3333   Primary smelting and refining of zinc
- 3334   Primary production of aluminum
- 3339   Primary smelting and refining of nonferrous metals not elsewhere classified

334   Secondary smelting and refining of nonferrous metals and alloys

335   Rolling, drawing, and extruding of nonferrous metals
- 3351   Rolling, drawing, and extruding of copper
- 3352   Rolling, drawing, and extruding of aluminum
- 3356   Rolling, drawing, and extruding of nonferrous metals, except copper and aluminum
- 3357   Drawing and insulating of nonferrous wire

336   Nonferrous foundries
- 3361   Aluminum castings
- 3362   Brass, bronze, copper, and copper base alloy castings
- 3369   Nonferrous castings not elsewhere classified

339   Miscellaneous primary metals industries
- 3391   Iron and steel forgings
- 3392   Nonferrous forgings
- 3399   Primary metal industries not elsewhere classified

34   Fabricated metals products, except ordnance, machinery, and transportation equipment   34

341   Metal cans

342   Cutlery, hand tools, and general hardware
    3421   Cutlery
    3423   Hand and edge tools, except machine tools and hand-
           saws
    3425   Handsaws and saw blades
    3429   Hardware not elsewhere classified

343   Heating apparatus (except electric) and plumbing fixtures
    3431   Enameled iron and metal sanitary ware
    3432   Plumbing fixture fittings and trim (brass goods)
    3433   Heating equipment, except electric

344   Fabricated structural metal products
    3441   Fabricated structural steel
    3442   Metal doors, sash, frames, molding, and trim
    3443   Fabricated platework (boiler shops)
    3444   Sheet metalwork
    3449   Architectural and miscellaneous metalwork

345   Screw machine products and bolts, nuts, screws, rivets, and
    washers
    3451   Screw machine products
    3452   Bolts, nuts, screws, rivets, and washers

346   Metal stampings

347   Coating, engraving, and allied services
    3471   Electroplating, plating, polishing, anodizing, and
           coloring
    3479   Coating, engraving, and allied services not else-
           where classified

348   Miscellaneous fabricated wire products

349   Miscellaneous fabricated metal products
    3491   Metal shipping barrels, drums, kegs, and pails
    3492   Safes and vaults
    3493   Steel springs
    3494   Valves and pipe fittings, except plumbers' brass
           goods
    3496   Collapsible tubes
    3497   Metal foil and leaf
    3498   Fabricated pipe and fabricated pipe fittings
    3499   Fabricated metal products not elsewhere classified

35   Machinery, except electrical   35

    351   Engines and turbines
        3511   Steam engines; steam, gas, and hydraulic turbines;
            and steam, gas, and hydraulic turbine generator set
            units
        3519   Internal combustion engines not elsewhere classified

    352   Farm machinery and equipment

    353   Construction, mining, and materials handling machinery
        and equipment

	3531	Construction machinery and equipment
	3532	Mining machinery and equipment, except oil field machinery and equipment
	3533	Oil field machinery and equipment
	3534	Elevators and moving stairways
	3535	Conveyors and conveying equipment
	3536	Hoists, industrial cranes, and monorail systems
	3537	Industrial trucks, tractors, trailers, and stackers
354		Metalworking machinery and equipment
	3541	Machine tools, metal cutting types
	3542	Machine tools, metal forming types
	3544	Special dies and tools, die sets, jigs, and fixtures
	3545	Machine tool accessories and measuring devices
	3548	Metalworking machinery, except machine tools
355		Special industry machinery, except metalworking machinery
	3551	Food products machinery
	3552	Textile machinery
	3553	Woodworking machinery
	3554	Paper industries machinery
	3555	Printing trades machinery and equipment
	3559	Special industry machinery not elsewhere classified
356		General industrial machinery and equipment
	3561	Pumps, air and gas compressors, and pumping equipment
	3562	Ball and roller bearings
	3564	Blowers and exhaust and ventilating fans
	3565	Industrial patterns
	3566	Mechanical power transmission equipment, except ball and roller bearings
	3567	Industrial process furnaces and ovens
	3569	General industrial machinery and equipment not elsewhere classified
357		Office, computing, and accounting machines
	3571	Computing and accounting machines, including cash registers
	3572	Typewriters
	3576	Scales and balances, except laboratory
	3579	Office machines not elsewhere classified
358		Service industries machines
	3581	Automatic merchandising machines
	3582	Commercial laundry, dry cleaning, and pressing machines
	3584	Vacuum cleaners, industrial
	3585	Refrigerators; refrigeration machinery, except household; and complete air conditioning units
	3586	Measuring and dispensing pumps
	3589	Service industry machines not elsewhere classified
359		Miscellaneous machinery, except electrical
	3591	Machine shops, jobbing and repair

3599 Machinery and parts, except electrical, not elsewhere classified

36 Electrical machinery, equipment, and supplies 36

361 Electric transmission and distribution equipment
3611 Electric measuring instruments and test equipment
3612 Power, distribution, and specialty transformers
3613 Switchgear and switchboard apparatus
3619 Electric transmission and distribution equipment not elsewhere classified

362 Electrical industrial apparatus
3621 Motors and generators
3622 Industrial controls
3623 Welding apparatus
3624 Carbon and graphite products
3629 Electrical industrial apparatus not elsewhere classified

363 Household appliances
3631 Household cooking equipment
3632 Household refrigerators and home and farm freezers
3633 Household laundry equipment
3634 Electric housewares and fans
3635 Household vacuum cleaners
3636 Sewing machines
3639 Household appliances not elsewhere classified

364 Electric lighting and wiring equipment
3641 Electric lamps
3642 Lighting fixtures
3643 Current carrying wiring devices
3644 Noncurrent carrying wiring devices

365 Radio and television receiving sets (except communication types) and phonograph records
3651 Radio and television receiving sets, except communication types
3652 Phonograph records

366 Communication equipment
3661 Telephone and telegraph apparatus
3662 Radio and television transmitting, signaling, and detection equipment and apparatus

367 Electronic components and accessories
3671 Radio and television receiving type electron tubes, except cathode ray
3672 Cathode ray picture tubes
3673 Transmitting, industrial, and special purpose electron tubes
3679 Electronic components and accessories not elsewhere classified

369 Miscellaneous electrical machinery, equipment, and supplies
3691 Storage batteries

3692   Primary batteries, dry and wet

3693   Radiographic X-ray, fluoroscopic X-ray, therapeutic X-ray, and other X-ray apparatus and tubes

3694   Electrical equipment for internal combustion engines

3699   Electrical machinery, equipment, and supplies not elsewhere classified

37   Transportation equipment   37

371   Motor vehicles and motor vehicle equipment
3711   Motor vehicles
3712   Passenger car bodies
3713   Truck and bus bodies
3714   Motor vehicle parts and accessories
3715   Truck trailers

372   Aircraft and parts
3721   Aircraft
3722   Aircraft engines and engine parts
3723   Aircraft propellers and propeller parts
3729   Aircraft parts and auxiliary equipment not elsewhere classified

373   Ship- and boat-building and repairing
3731   Shipbuilding and repairing
3732   Boatbuilding and repairing

374   Railroad equipment
3741   Locomotives and parts
3742   Railroad and street cars

375   Motorcycles, bicycles, and parts

379   Miscellaneous transportation equipment
3791   Trailer coaches
3799   Transportation equipment not elsewhere classified

38   Professional, scientific, and controlling instruments; photographic and optical goods; watches and clocks   38

381   Engineering, laboratory, and scientific and research instruments and associated equipment

382   Instruments for measuring, controlling, and indicating physical characteristics
3821   Mechanical measuring and controlling instruments, except automatic temperature controls
3822   Automatic temperature controls

383   Optical instruments and lenses

384   Surgical, medical, and dental instruments and supplies
3841   Surgical and medical instruments and apparatus
3842   Orthopedic, prosthetic, and surgical appliances and supplies
3843   Dental equipment and supplies

385   Ophthalmic goods

386   Photographic equipment and supplies

387   Watches, clocks, and clockwork operated devices; parts
    3871   Watches, clocks, and parts except watchcases
    3872   Watchcases

39   Miscellaneous manufacturing industries 39

391   Jewelry, silverware, and plated ware
    3911   Jewelry, precious metal
    3912   Jewelers' findings and materials
    3913   Lapidary work and cutting and polishing diamonds
    3914   Silverware and plated ware

393   Musical instruments and parts

394   Toys and amusement, sporting, and athletic goods
    3941   Games and toys, except dolls and children's vehicles
    3942   Dolls
    3943   Children's vehicles, except bicycles
    3949   Sporting and athletic goods not elsewhere classified

395   Pens, pencils, and other office and artists' materials
    3951   Pens, pen points, fountain pens, ball-point pens, and
           mechanical pencils and parts
    3952   Lead pencils, crayons, and artists' materials
    3953   Marking devices
    3955   Carbon paper and inked ribbons

396   Costume jewelry, costume novelties, buttons, and miscel-
    laneous notions, except precious metal
    3961   Costume jewelry and costume novelties, except pre-
           cious metal
    3962   Feathers, plumes, and artificial flowers
    3963   Buttons
    3964   Needles, pins, hooks and eyes, and similar notions

398   Miscellaneous manufacturing industries 398, 399
    3981   Brooms and brushes
    3982   Linoleum, asphalted felt base, and other hard sur-
           face floor covering not elsewhere classified
    3983   Matches
    3984   Lamp shades 3987
    3985   Morticians' goods 3988
    3986   Furs, dressed and dyed 3992
    3987   Signs and advertising displays 3993
    3988   Umbrellas, parasols, and canes 3995
    3989   Manufacturing industries not elsewhere classified .. 3999

399   Ordnance and accessories 19
    3991   Guns, howitzers, mortars, and related equipment... 191
    3992   Ammunition, except for small arms 192
    3993   Tanks and tank components 193
    3994   Sighting and fire control equipment 194
    3995   Small arms 195
    3996   Small arms ammunition 196
    3999   Ordnance and accessories not elsewhere classified .. 199

432   Highway rights of way

439   Transportation rights of way not elsewhere classified

44   Water and pipeline transportation 44, 46

441   Deep sea foreign transportation

442   Deep sea domestic transportation
  4421   Transportation to and between noncontiguous territories
  4422   Coastwise transportation
  4423   Intercoastal transportation

443   Great Lakes - St. Lawrence Seaway transportation

444   Transportation on rivers and canals

445   Local water transportation
  4452   Ferries
  4453   Lighterage
  4454   Towing and tugboat service
  4459   Local water transportation not elsewhere classified

446   Services incidental to water transportation
  4462   Piers and docks
  4463   Stevedoring
  4464   Canal operation
  4469   Water transportation services not elsewhere classified

447   Petroleum pipelines 461
  4472   Crude petroleum pipelines 4612
  4473   Refined petroleum pipelines 4613

45   Air transportation 45

451   Air transportation, certificated carriers

452   Air transportation, noncertificated carriers

453   Fixed facilities and services related to air transportation . . 458
  4532   Airports and flying fields 4582
  4533   Airport terminal services 4583

458   Other air transportation services 47

46   Warehousing, public and private 422

461   Farm product warehousing and storage 4221

462   Refrigerated warehousing, except food lockers 4222

463   Food lockers, with or without food preparation facilities . . 4223

464   Household goods warehousing and storage 4224

465   General warehousing and storage 4225

466   Special warehousing and storage not elsewhere classified . . 4226

47   Rights of way, utilities . . . . - - -

5   COMMERCIAL

5028 Paints and varnishes
5029 Chemicals and allied products not elsewhere classified

503 Dry goods and apparel
5032 Dry goods, piece goods, and notions
5035 Apparel and accessories, hosiery, and lingerie
5039 Footwear

504 Groceries and related products
5042 Groceries, general line
5043 Dairy products
5044 Poultry and poultry products
5045 Confectionery
5046 Fish and seafoods
5047 Meats and meat products
5048 Fresh fruits and vegetables
5049 Groceries and related products not elsewhere classified

505 Farm products—raw materials

506 Electrical goods
5062 Electrical merchandise, general line
5063 Electrical apparatus and equipment, wiring supplies, and construction materials
5064 Electrical appliances and television and radio sets
5065 Electronic parts and equipment

507 Hardware, and plumbing and heating, and air conditioning and refrigeration equipment and supplies
5072 Hardware
5074 Plumbing and heating equipment and supplies
5077 Air conditioning and refrigeration equipment and supplies

508 Machinery, equipment, and supplies
5082 Commercial and industrial machinery, equipment, and supplies
5083 Farm machinery and equipment
5086 Professional equipment and supplies
5087 Equipment and supplies for service establishments
5088 Transportation equipment and supplies, except motor vehicles
5089 Machinery, equipment, and supplies not elsewhere classified

509 Miscellaneous wholesalers
5094 Tobacco and tobacco products
5095 Beer, wine, and distilled alcoholic beverages
5096 Paper and paper products
5097 Furniture and home furnishings
5098 Lumber and construction materials
5099 Wholesalers not elsewhere classified

52 Retail trade—building materials, hardware, and farm equipment 52

521 Lumber and other building materials dealers
  5211 Lumberyards
  5212 Building materials dealers, except lumberyards

522 Heating and plumbing equipment dealers

523 Paint, glass, and wallpaper stores

524 Electrical supply stores

525 Hardware and farm equipment
  5251 Hardware stores
  5252 Farm equipment dealers

53 Retail trade—general merchandise 53

531 Department stores

532 Mail order houses
  5322 Mail order houses, general merchandise
  5323 Mail order houses, except general merchandise

533 Limited price variety stores

534 Merchandise vending machine operators
  5341 Automatic merchandising

535 Direct selling organizations

539 Miscellaneous general merchandise stores
  5392 Dry goods and general merchandise stores
  5393 General stores

54 Retail trade—food 54

541 Grocery stores and delicatessens

542 Meat and fish (seafood) markets
  5422 Meat markets
  5423 Fish (seafood) markets

543 Fruit stores and vegetable markets

544 Candy, nut, and confectionery stores

545 Dairy products stores

546 Retail bakeries
  5462 Retail bakeries, manufacturing
  5463 Retail bakeries, nonmanufacturing

549 Miscellaneous food stores
  5491 Egg and poultry dealers
  5499 Food stores not elsewhere classified

55 Automotive dealers and gasoline service stations 55

551 Motor vehicle dealers, new and used

552 Motor vehicle dealers, used only

553 Tire, battery, and accessory dealers

554   Gasoline service stations

555   Mobile home dealers, new and used . . . .   - - -

559   Miscellaneous aircraft, marine, and automotive dealers

56   Retail trade—apparel and accessories   56

    561   Men's and boys' clothing and furnishings stores
        5612   Men's and boys' clothing stores
        5613   Men's and boys' furnishings stores

    562   Women's ready-to-wear stores

    563   Women's accessory and specialty stores
        5631   Millinery stores
        5632   Corset and lingerie stores
        5633   Hosiery stores
        5634   Apparel accessory and other specialty stores

    564   Children's and infants' wear stores

    565   Family clothing stores

    566   Shoe stores
        5662   Men's shoe stores
        5663   Women's shoe stores
        5664   Children's and juveniles' shoe stores
        5665   Family shoe stores

    567   Custom tailors

    568   Furriers and fur shops

    569   Miscellaneous apparel and accessory stores

57   Retail trade—furniture, home furnishings, and equipment   57

    571   Furniture, home furnishings, and equipment stores
        5712   Furniture stores
        5713   Floor covering stores
        5714   Drapery, curtain, and upholstery stores
        5715   China, glassware, and metalware stores
        5719   Miscellaneous home furnishings stores

    572   Household appliance stores

    573   Radio, television, and music stores

58   Retail trade—eating and drinking places   58

    581   Eating and drinking places
        5812   Eating places
        5813   Drinking places (alcoholic beverages)
        5814   Combination bars and restaurants . . . .   - - -

59   Retail trade—miscellaneous retail stores   59

    591   Drugstores and proprietary stores

    592   Liquor stores

593   Antique stores and secondhand stores
    5932   Antique stores
    5933   Secondhand clothing and shoe stores
    5934   Secondhand furniture stores
    5935   Secondhand bookstores
    5936   Secondhand automotive tire, battery, and accessory dealers
    5939   Secondhand stores not elsewhere classified

594   Bookstores and stationery stores
    5942   Bookstores
    5943   Stationery stores

595   Sporting goods stores and bicycle shops
    5952   Sporting goods stores
    5953   Bicycle shops

596   Farm and garden supply stores
    5962   Hay, grain, and feed stores
    5969   Farm and garden supply stores not elsewhere classified

597   Jewelry stores

598   Fuel and ice dealers
    5982   Fuel dealers, except fuel oil dealers
    5983   Fuel oil and bottled gas dealers
    5984   Ice dealers

599   Retail stores not elsewhere classified
    5992   Florists
    5993   Tobacco stores
    5994   News dealers and newsstands
    5996   Camera and photographic supply stores
    5997   Gift, novelty, and souvenir shops
    5998   Optical goods stores
    5999   Miscellaneous retail stores not elsewhere classified

6   PERSONAL, BUSINESS, AND PROFESSIONAL SERVICES

60   Finance, insurance, and real estate ....   - - -

601   Credit agencies other than banks   61
    6011   Rediscount and financing institutions for credit agencies other than banks   611
    6012   Savings and loan associations   612
    6013   Agricultural credit institutions   613
    6014   Personal credit institutions, including credit unions   614
    6015   Business credit institutions, including mortgages..   615
    6016   Loan correspondents and brokers   616

602   Security and commodity brokers, dealers, exchanges, and services   62
    6021   Security brokers, dealers, and flotation companies..   621
    6022   Commodity contracts, brokers and dealers   622

COMMITTEE   SIC
CODE NO.   CODE NO.

616   Funeral service and crematories 726

617   Pressing, alteration, and garment repair 727
  6171   Pressing, alteration, and garment repair, except fur   7271
  6172   Fur repair and storage 7272

619   Miscellaneous personal services 729

62 Miscellaneous business services 73

621   Advertising 731
  6211   Advertising agencies, except outdoor 7311
  6212   Outdoor advertising services 7312
  6219   Miscellaneous advertising 7319

622   Consumer credit reporting agencies, mercantile reporting agencies, and adjustment and collection agencies 732

623   Duplicating, addressing, blueprinting, photocopying, mailing, mailing list, and stenographic services 733
  6231   Duplicating, addressing, mailing, mailing list, and stenographic services 7331
  6232   Blueprinting and photocopying services 7332

624   Services to dwellings and other buildings 734
  6241   Window cleaning 7341
  6242   Disinfecting and exterminating services 7342
  6249   Miscellaneous services to dwellings and other buildings 7349

625   News syndicates 735

626   Private employment agencies 736

629   Business services not elsewhere classified 739
  6291   Research, development, and testing laboratories.... 7391
  6292   Business and management consulting services 7392
  6299   Business services not elsewhere classified 7399

63 Automobile repair, services, and garages 75

631   Automobile rentals, without drivers, and driveaways 751

632   Automobile parking 752
  6321   Parking lots 7521
  6322   Parking structures 7522

633   Automobile repair shops 753
  6331   Top and body repair shops 7531
  6332   Battery and ignition repair and service shops 7532
  6333   Radiator repair shops 7533
  6334   Tire repair shops 7534
  6335   Paint shops 7535
  6336   Glass replacement and repair shops 7536
  6338   General automobile repair shops 7538
  6339   Automobile repair shops not elsewhere classified... 7539

634   Automobile services, except repair (includes auto wash).. 754

635   Trailer rentals 751

COMMITTEE CODE NO.			SIC CODE NO.

7   PUBLIC AND QUASI-PUBLIC SERVICES .... - - -

70   Postal services 91

71   Military services 91

72   Other federal government 91

73   State, county, and local government 92, 93

    731   State government 92

    732   County government 93

    733   Local government 93

    734   *Ad hoc* governmental agencies .... - - -

74   Public schools 82

    741   Public colleges and universities 8221

    742   Public junior colleges 8222

    743   Public high schools 821

    744   Public junior high schools 821

    745   Public elementary schools 821

    749   Public schools not elsewhere classified 829

75   Private schools 82

    751   Private colleges and universities 8221

    752   Private junior colleges 8222

    753   Private high schools 821

    754   Private junior high schools 821

    755   Private elementary schools 821

    756   Private nursery schools 821

    757   Private correspondence and vocational schools 824

    759   Private schools not elsewhere classified 829

76   Museums, art galleries, arboreta, libraries, churches, and cemeteries .... - - -

    761   Museums and art galleries 841

    762   Arboreta, botanical and zoological gardens 842

    763   Libraries 823

    764   Churches 866

    765   Religious services not elsewhere classified .... - - -

    766   Cultural services not elsewhere classified .... - - -

COMMITTEE CODE NO.		SIC CODE NO.
	813 Fishing sites	- - -
	814 Swimming pools, outdoor	- - -
82	Indoor public recreation	- - -
	821 Swimming pools	- - -
	822 Arenas	- - -
	823 Skating rinks	- - -
	824 Community centers	- - -
83	Outdoor private land recreation (operated for profit)	- - -
	831 Stadia	- - -
	832 Race tracks	7948
	833 Camps and campgrounds	7032
	834 Riding academies	7946
	835 Skating rinks	7945
	836 Ski and toboggan runs	- - -
	837 Gun clubs	- - -
84	Outdoor water-based private recreation	
	841 Boating areas	- - -
	842 Bathing beaches	7943
	843 Fishing sites	- - -
	844 Swimming pools, outdoor	7944
85	Indoor private recreation	
	851 Swimming pools	7944
	852 Arenas	- - -
	853 Skating rinks	7945
86	Open lands	- - -
	861 Conservation lands	- - -
	862 Wildlife areas	- - -
	863 Forest preserves	- - -
87	Private nonprofit recreation	- - -
	871 Subdivision parks	- - -
	872 Subdivision community centers	- - -
	873 Camps (Boy Scout, etc.)	- - -
	874 Golf courses, country clubs, etc.	7942, 7947
	875 Gun clubs	- - -
	879 Private nonprofit recreation not elsewhere classified	- - -